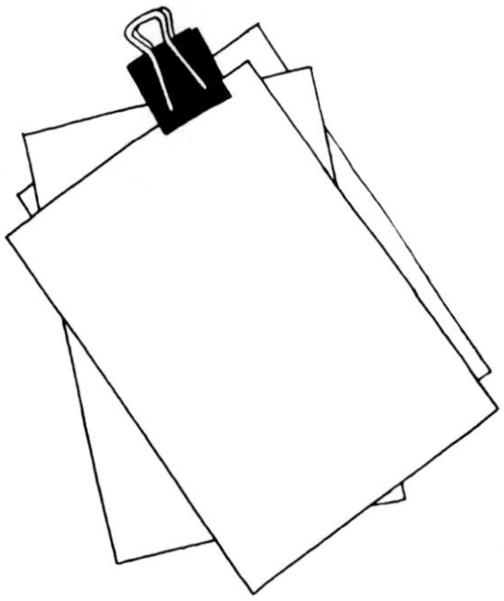

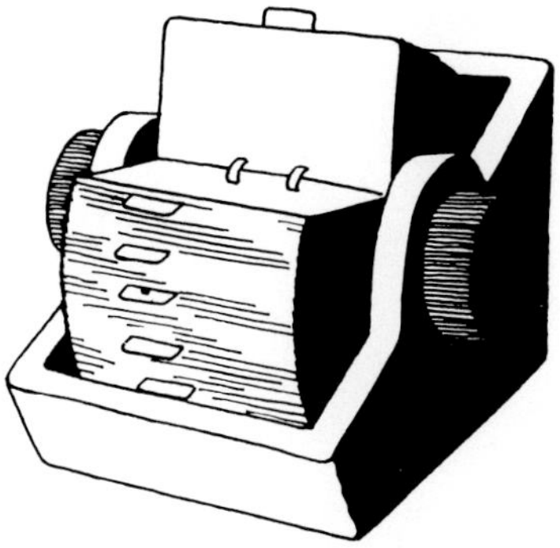

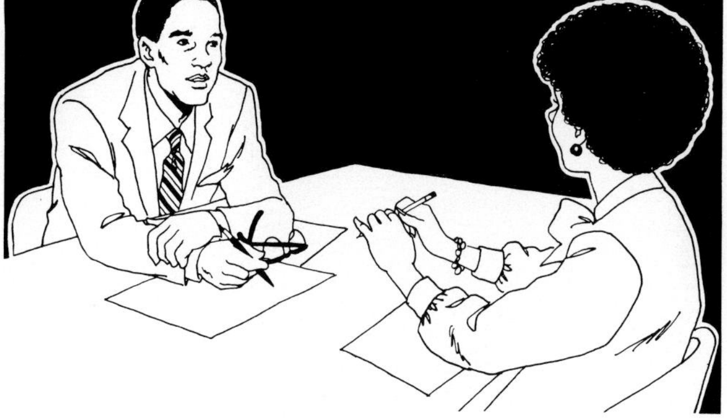

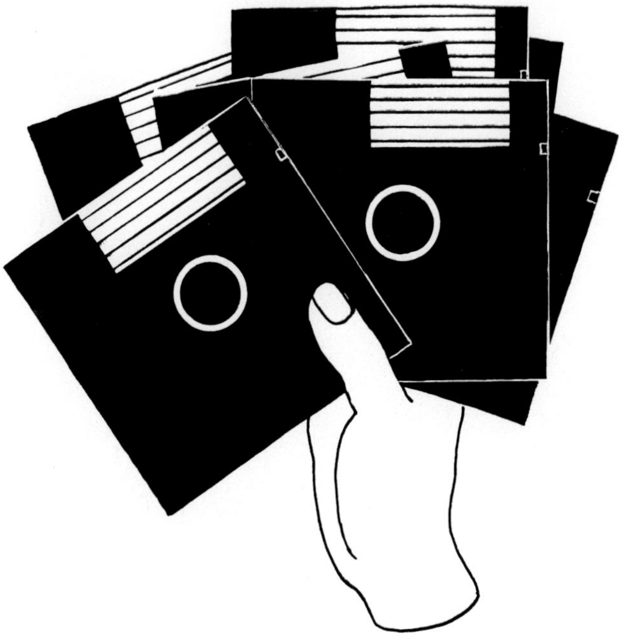

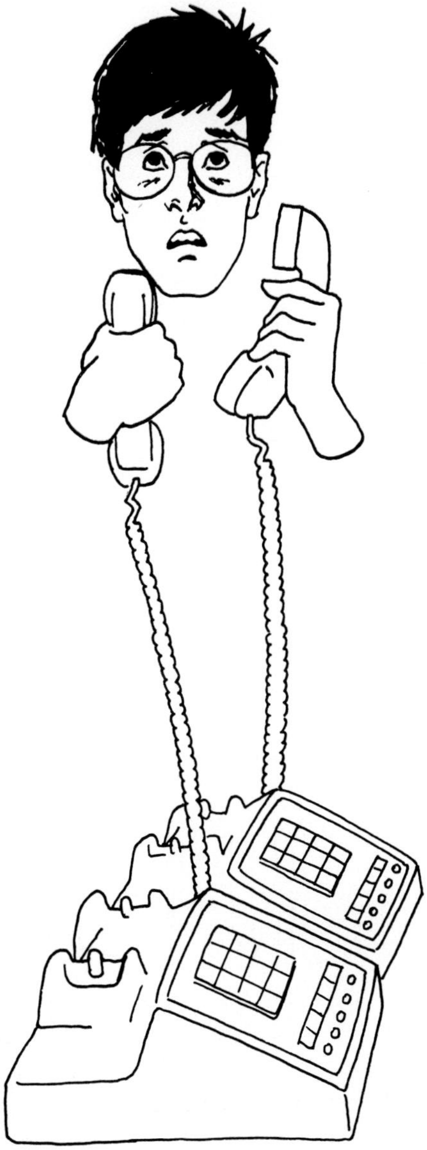

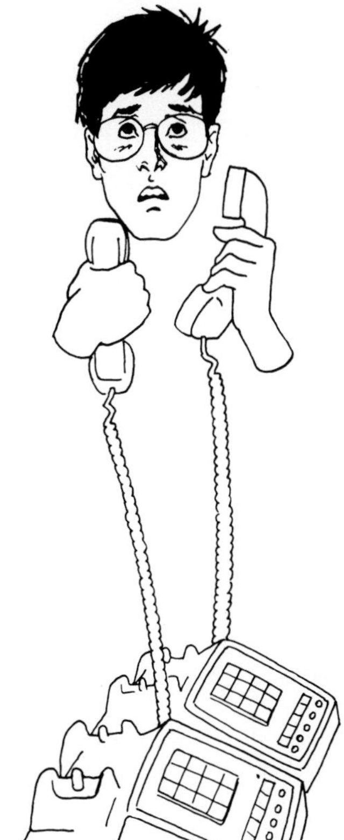

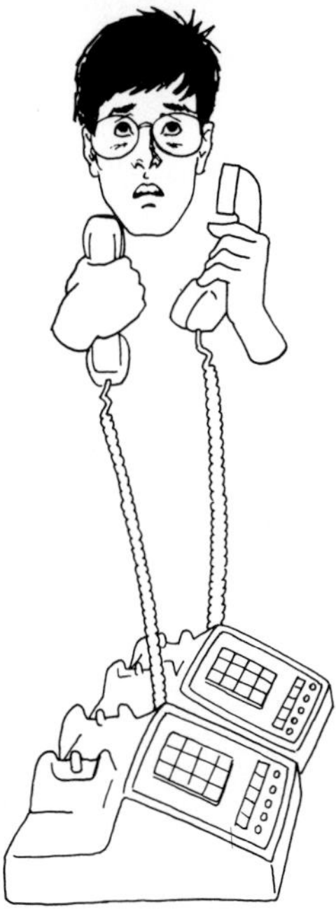

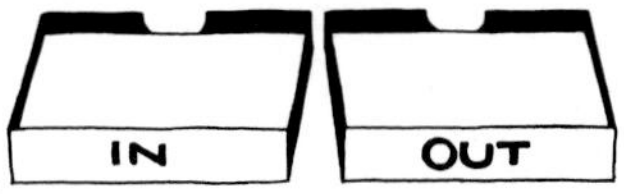
IN
OUT

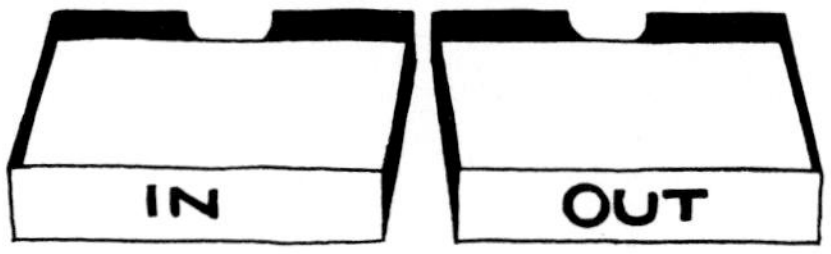
IN
OUT

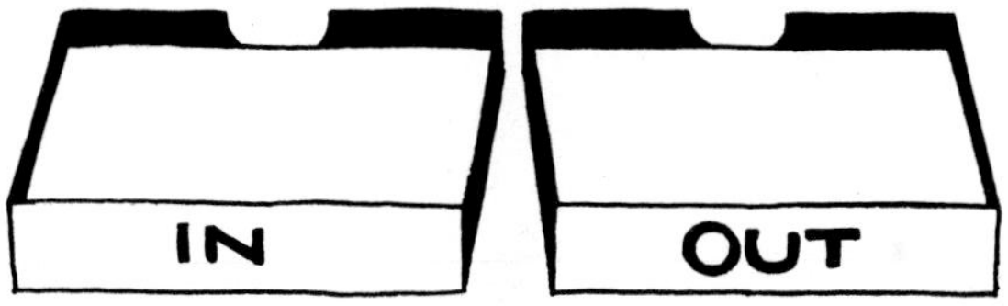
IN
OUT

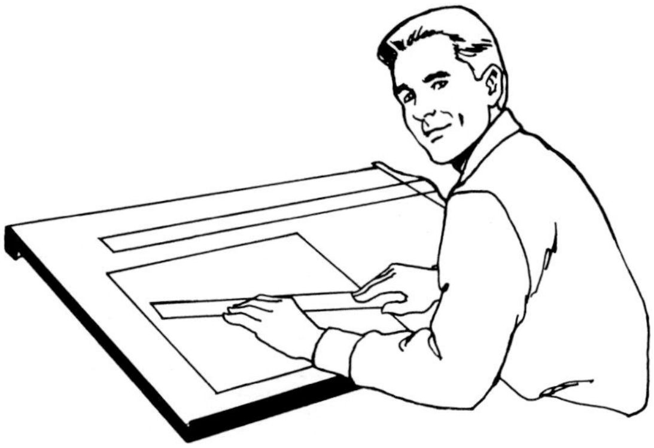
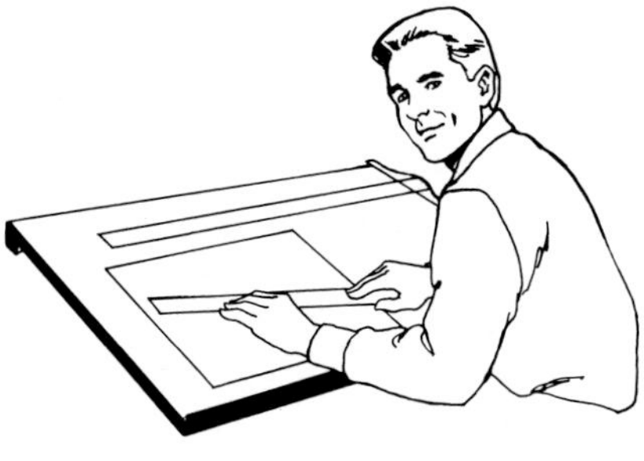
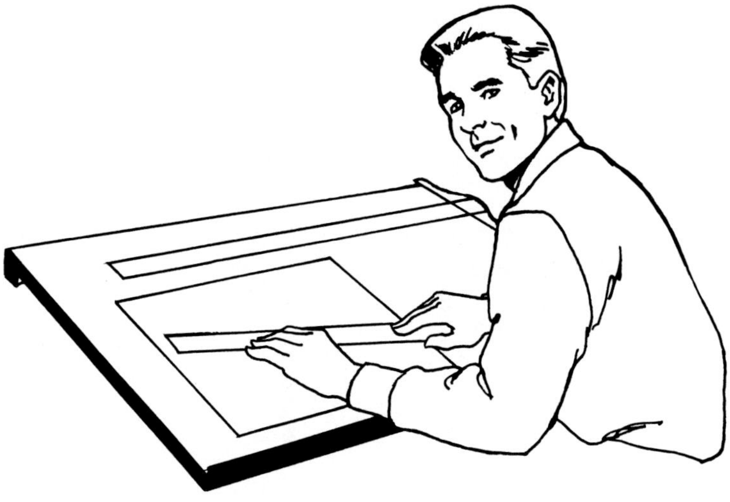

BULLETINS

BULLETINS

BULLETINS

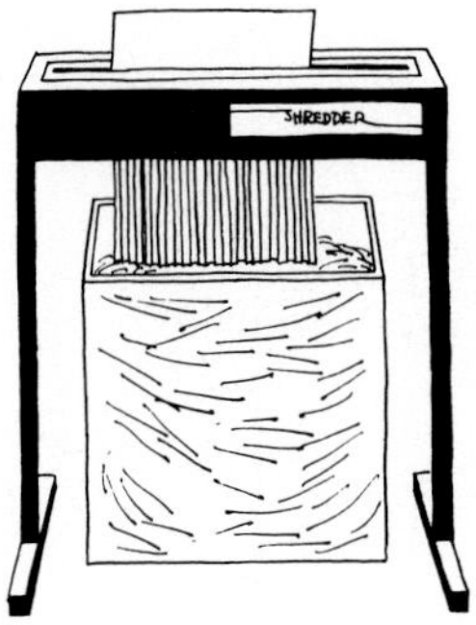
SHREDDER

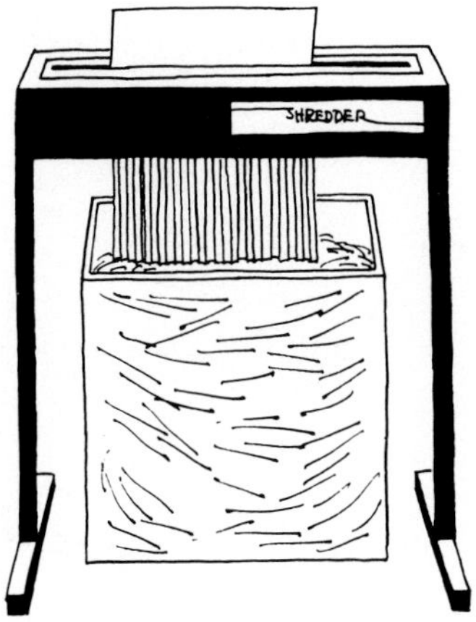
SHREDDER

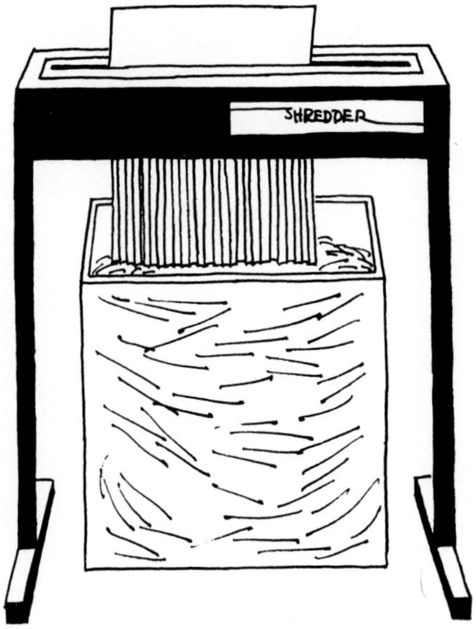
SHREDDER

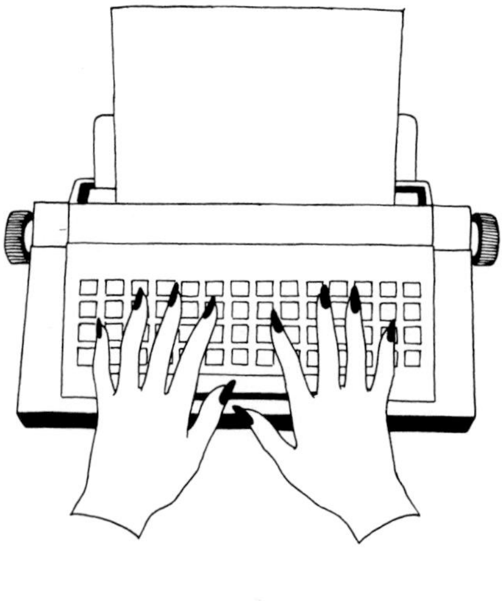

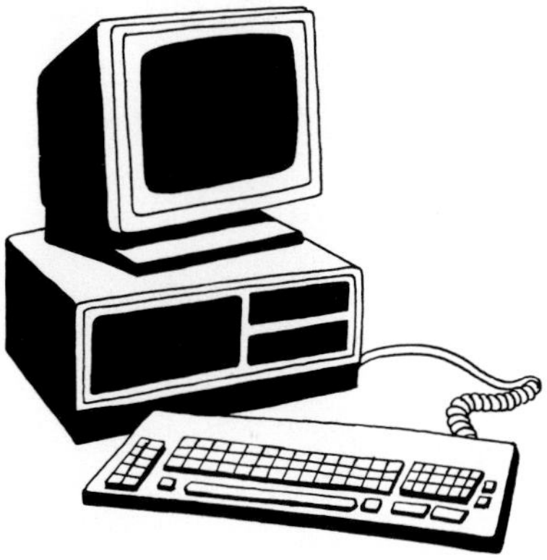

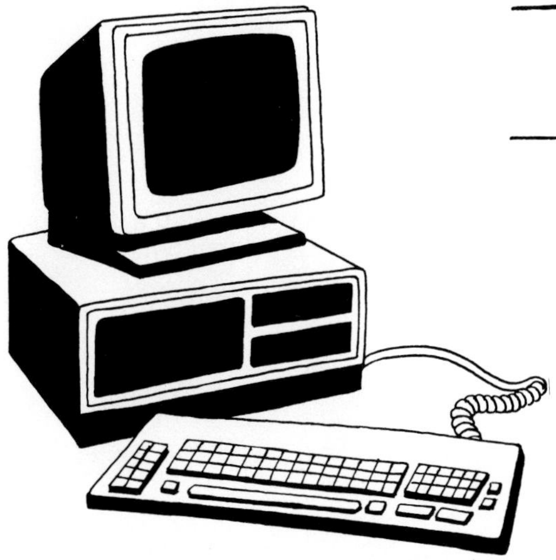

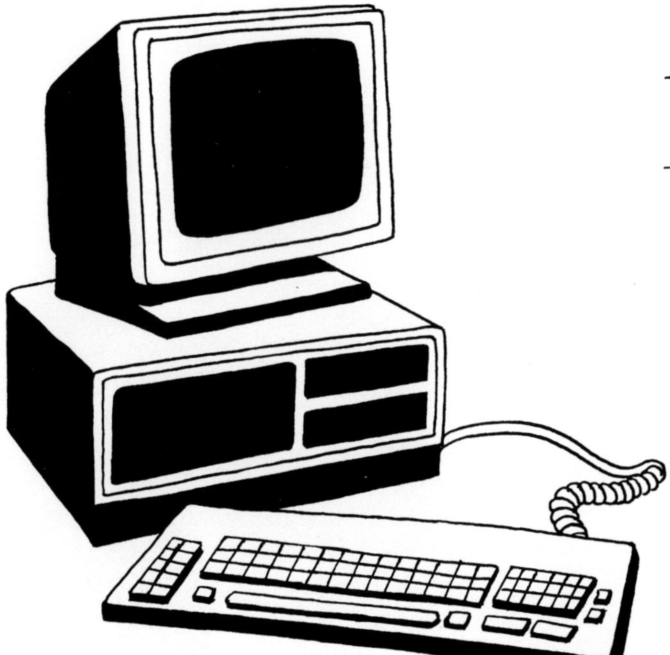

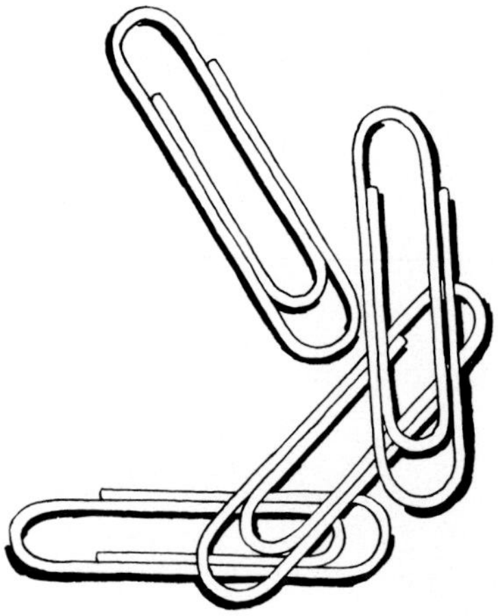

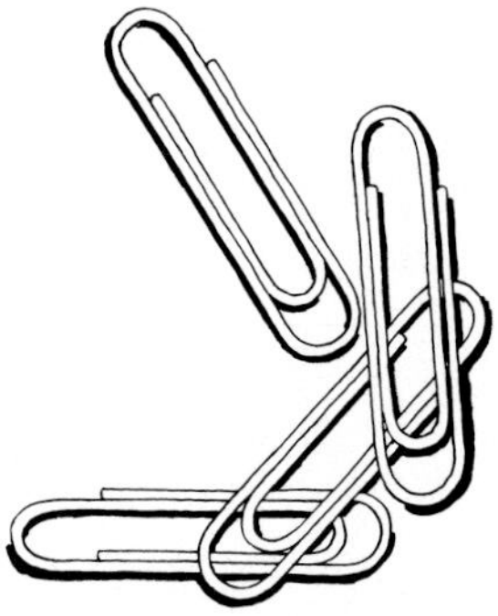

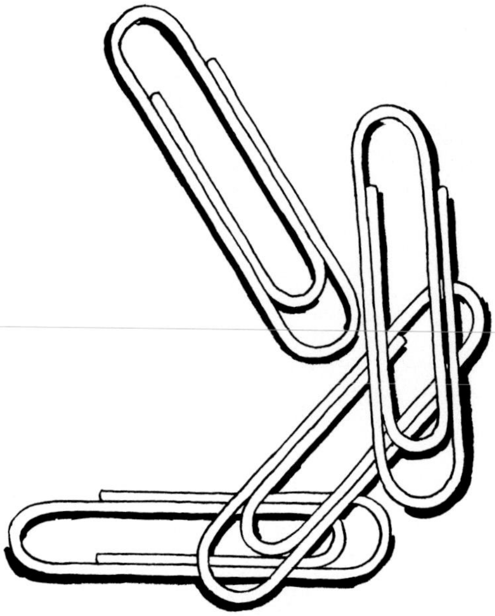

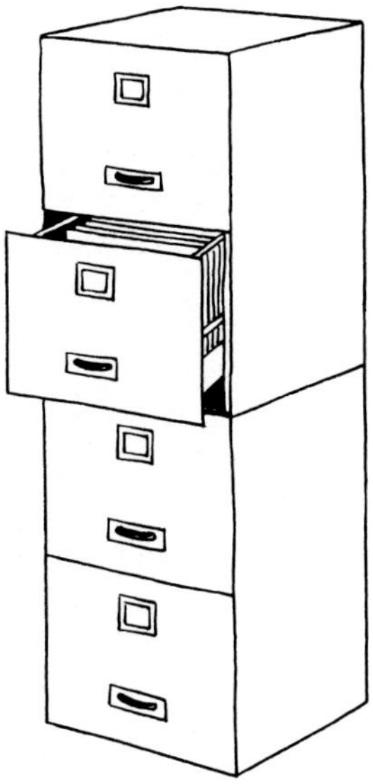
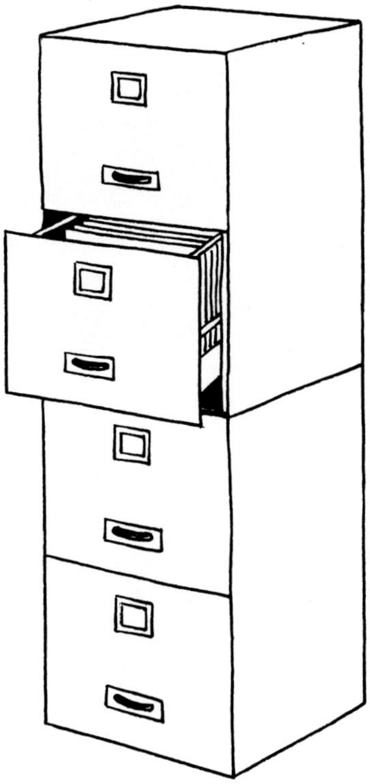

APPROVED

APPROVED

APPROVED

REJECT

REJECT

REJECT

IN

IN

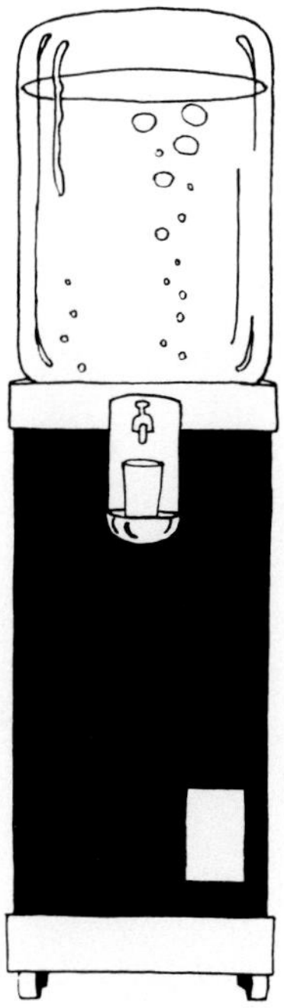

RUSH

RUSH

RUSH